ℒENT *and* ℰASTER ⟊ISDOM
──── *from* ────
G. K. CHESTERTON

Daily Scripture and Prayers Together
With G. K. Chesterton's Own Words

The Center for the Study
of C. S. Lewis and Friends

Compilation, Prayers, and Actions by
Thom Satterlee and Robert Moore-Jumonville

Liguori
LIGUORI, MISSOURI

Imprimi Potest:
Thomas D. Picton, C.Ss.R.
Provincial, Denver Province
The Redemptorists

Published by Liguori Publications
Liguori, Missouri 63057-9999
www.liguori.org

Compilation, Prayers, and Actions by Thom Satterlee and Robert Moore-Jumonville

Library of Congress Cataloging-in-Publication Data

Chesterton, G. K. (Gilbert Keith), 1874–1936.
    Lent and Easter wisdom from G. K. Chesterton : daily scripture and prayers together with G. K. Chesterton's own words / compiled by Thom Satterlee and Robert Moore-Jumonville. — 1st ed.
        p. cm. — (Lent and Easter wisdom)
    ISBN 978-0-7648-1698-7
    1. Lent—Prayers and devotions. 2. Easter—Prayers and devotions. I. Satterlee, Thom. II. Moore-Jumonville, Robert. III. Title.
    BV85.C473 2008
    242'.34—dc22   2007038854

Liguori Publications, a nonprofit corporation, is an apostolate of the Redemptorists. To learn more about the Redemptorists, visit Redemptorists.com.

Printed in the United States of America
11   5 4 3 2

Contents

Introduction

GILBERT KEITH CHESTERTON (1874–1936) never went to college. After his early education at St. Paul's, he attended Slade Art School in London, only later to become a journalist and writer. His educational and vocational experiences combined to develop in him a remarkable interdisciplinary intelligence, though Chesterton claimed with a grin that he succeeded as a journalist mainly by failing to become an artist. "Journalist," in fact, is how he normally described himself.

It is more accurate, however, to call Chesterton a Christian cultural critic. He was an intellectual who wrote broadly in defense of Christian culture in the late-nineteenth-century "man of letters" tradition. He employed a variety of genres: poetry, biography, literary criticism, novel, short story, apologetics, and even mysteries. His mysteries include the much-loved figure of Father Brown, and his novels often convey a Monty Pythonesque sense of absurd humor. Many of Chesterton's poems rank among the finest English poetry, and his nonfiction also has received high praise. The great Thomistic authority Etienne Gilson maintained that no scholar could have written the biography of Aquinas that Chesterton wrote: "He has guessed all that which they had tried to demonstrate, and he has said all that which they were more or less clumsily attempting to express in academic formulas."

Throughout his life, Chesterton debated towering intellectuals such as Bernard Shaw, H. G. Wells, and Bertrand Russell, but he always conducted his arguments with respect and appreciation for the other as a person. In a memorable correspondence between Chesterton and the atheist H. G. Wells, Chesterton suggested that the world had not been grateful enough for the literary gifts bestowed by Wells. Wells replied, with gratitude, that if he were to get into heaven, it would be as a friend of G. K. Chesterton's. In a subsequent letter, Chesterton teased Wells that he should be worried about whether or not he would get into heaven, but if he did, it would be not as a friend of Chesterton but as a friend of humankind. Such was Chesterton's spirit of largess, even with opponents.

Chesterton was, in fact, a loving genius, a man of great spiritual depth, with a terrific sense of humor—who thought we ought to have more time for serious work, like pasting colored tinsel on the cardboard figures of a toy theater. After reading even a little Chesterton, one is struck by his theology of joy, which he connects to sub-themes of wonder, gratitude, and appreciation. "There is no sense in not appreciating things," insisted Chesterton, "and there is no sense in having more of them if you have less appreciation of them."

If we could really fathom the gift of sheer existence, Chesterton tells us, our response would be one of gratitude—of surprise and wonder at simple, ordinary objects; experiences; and above all, people. May G. K. Chesterton serve us as our mentor and spiritual guide through this Lenten and Easter season.

ROBERT MOORE-JUMONVILLE
SPRING ARBOR UNIVERSITY
2007

PART I

~~~~~~

READINGS *for* LENT

DAY 1

Frenzied Asceticism

The essential difference between Christian and Pagan asceticism lies in the fact that Paganism in renouncing pleasure gives up something which it does not think desirable; whereas Christianity in giving up pleasure gives up something it thinks very desirable indeed. Thus there is a frenzy in Christian asceticism; its follies and renunciations are like those of first love.

G. F. WATTS

SPIRITUAL WORSHIP

I appeal to you therefore, brothers and sisters, by the mercies of God, to present your bodies as a living sacrifice, holy and acceptable to God, which is your spiritual worship.

ROMANS 12:1

PRAYER

Father, we offer to you only what we have been given from you: our bodies and our selves. Show us how we can worship you through the use of our bodies and the giving of ourselves. We want to live for others, as your Son has taught us.

LENTEN ACTION

It seems odd that we should give up pleasures that we consider good. But perhaps Chesterton's point in the quotation above is that we are always free to give up these pleasures and at times are drawn to do so out of love for others. As you go through your day today, think of pleasures you would like to give up for the sake of another. Would you miss an hour of sleep to speak with someone who needs your attention? Is there something else that you love but are willing to give up because you love some other person even more?

DAY 2

A Chance to Change

I want you to give them back, Flambeau, and I want you to give up this life. There is still youth and honor and humor in you; don't fancy they will last in that trade. Men may keep a sort of level of good, but no man has ever been able to keep on one level of evil. That road goes down and down. The kind man drinks and turns cruel; the frank man kills and lies about it. Many a man I've known started like you to be an honest outlaw, a merry robber of the rich, and ended stamped into slime. Maurice Blum started out as an anarchist of principle, a father of the poor; he ended a greasy spy and tale-bearer that both sides used and despised. Harry Burke started his free money movement sincerely enough; now he's sponging on a half-starved sister for endless brandies and sodas. Lord Amber went into wild society in a sort of chivalry; now he's paying blackmail to the lowest vultures in London. Captain Barillon was the great gentleman-apache before your time; he died in a madhouse, screaming with fear of the "narks" and receivers that had betrayed him and hunted him down. I know the woods look very free behind you, Flambeau; I know that in a flash you could melt into them like a monkey. But some day you will be an old grey monkey, Flambeau. You will sit up in your free forest cold at heart and close to death, and the tree-tops will be very bare."

THE INNOCENCE OF FATHER BROWN

GOOD NEWS

Now after John was arrested, Jesus came to Galilee, proclaiming the good news of God, and saying, "The time is fulfilled, and the kingdom of God has come near; repent, and believe in the good news."

MARK 1:14–15

So if anyone is in Christ, there is a new creation: everything old has passed away; see, everything has become new!

2 CORINTHIANS 5:17

PRAYER

God, if left to myself, I will always only act selfishly— in the service of my own devices and desires. But with your help, I can amend my life; I have hope of change. All things are possible with you; with you beside me, all things in me can be refashioned in Christ. What is dim can be enlightened. What is bent can be straightened. What is sick can be healed. Come, Lord: I want to be fresh clay for you to shape.

LENTEN ACTION

Ask yourself who you are becoming. A year from now will you be a better person or a worse one? If, indeed, we are to be made holy before we can face a holy God, shouldn't we start now? Plan to eliminate one vice from your life this year while adding one virtue.

DAY 3

Criticism Like God's

A good critic should be like God in the great saying of a Scottish mystic. George MacDonald said that God was easy to please and hard to satisfy. That paradox is the poise of all good artistic appreciation.

FANCIES VERSUS FADS

SOMETIMES PLEASING, SELDOM PERFECT

Do not neglect to do good and to share what you have, for such sacrifices are pleasing to God.

HEBREWS 13:16

"Be perfect, therefore, as your heavenly Father is perfect."

MATTHEW 5:48

PRAYER

Heavenly Father, we know we can always do more to please you. Help us to see this fact as a cause for celebration, a reason to delight in the work you give us; may we not be pressed down by our responsibilities but be lifted up by them, for in doing your will we draw closer to you, closer to joy.

LENTEN ACTION

Are you familiar with George MacDonald, the writer mentioned in today's passage by Chesterton? MacDonald was a great influence on Chesterton and many other Christian writers, including C. S. Lewis and J. R. R. Tolkien. If you are on the Internet today, look up a brief biography of George MacDonald. If your interest is piqued, buy or borrow one of his many books.

DAY 4

Virtues for Practice

*T*he human race has always admired the Catholic virtues, however little it can practice them; and oddly enough it has admired most those of them that the modern world most sharply disputes."

MacIan, in *The Ball and the Cross*

Living Faith

...[P]ursue righteousness, godliness, faith, love, endurance, gentleness.

1 Timothy 6:11

Prayer

Teach us spiritual virtues, Heavenly Father. Hold before our minds the example of your Son. Open us to the gentle nudges of your Holy Spirit.

LENTEN ACTION

Consider the six virtues found in the reading from First Timothy: righteousness, godliness, faith, love, endurance, and gentleness. Look over these words and ask yourself how you might increase your practice of one of these virtues today, this week, or this month.

DAY 5

Tired and Thirsty

All men thirst to confess their crimes more than tired beasts thirst for water; but they naturally object to confessing them while other people, who have also committed the same crimes, sit by and laugh at them.

"PUBLIC CONFESSIONS BY POLITICIANS,"
ILLUSTRATED LONDON NEWS, MARCH 14, 1908

CONFESS YOUR SINS

The prayer of faith will save the sick, and the Lord will raise them up; and anyone who has committed sins will be for-given. Therefore confess your sins to one another, and pray for one another, so that you may be healed. The prayer of the righteous is powerful and effective.

JAMES 5:15–16

PRAYER

Lord, I confess to you. I have sinned against you and against my neighbors in ways obvious to me and in ways of which I am unaware. Wash me, Lord, and I will be clean. Through the precious blood Jesus, my Savior, shed on the cross to take away the sins of the world, blot out my offenses. I believe, merciful Lord, not only that my past sins can be erased as far as you are concerned but also that you might plant in me the seeds of a new and right spirit. Lead me, Lord, to a priest or trusted friend with whom to share my confession.

LENTEN ACTION

With some friends, watch the clip from the film *The Mission* in which Robert De Niro's character, Rodrigo Mendoza, climbs the falls carrying a heavy burden as a means of penance. Discuss your interpretation of the scene together. What actions could you take, what good deeds could you perform, as a symbol of your sorrow for your sins? If you are Catholic, go to confession this week. If you are not, find a trusted spiritual mentor or friend with whom to share your confession of sin.

DAY 6

Loving the World Enough to Change It

What we need is not the cold acceptance of the world as a compromise, but some way in which we can heartily hate and heartily love it. We do not want joy and anger to neutralize each other and produce a surly contentment; we want a fiercer delight and a fiercer discontent. We have to feel the universe at once as an ogre's castle, to be stormed, and yet as our own cottage, to which we can return at evening.

No one doubts that an ordinary man can get on with this world….[But] can he hate it enough to change it, and yet love it enough to think it worth changing?

ORTHODOXY

THE SPIRIT OF THE LORD

When he came to Nazareth, where he had been brought up, he went to the synagogue on the sabbath day, as was his custom. He stood up to read, and the scroll of the prophet Isaiah was given to him. He unrolled the scroll and found the place where it was written:

"The Spirit of the Lord is upon me,
because he has anointed me
to bring good news to the poor.
He has sent me to proclaim release to the captives
and recovery of sight to the blind,
to let the oppressed go free,
to proclaim the year of the Lord's favor."

And he rolled up the scroll, gave it back to the attendant, and sat down. The eyes of all in the synagogue were fixed on him.

LUKE 4:16–20

PRAYER

Show me, God, Protector of the Poor, from where social justice originates. Lead me to recognize that because you are within my neighbor, my neighbor and I are essentially one—bound together in you. Teach me to look past race, ethnicity, social status, party labels, and physical challenges to see the human within my neighbor. And who is my neighbor? Lead me toward empathy for and solidarity with all those in the world who are suffering. Show me, most merciful God, that justice originates within you—with your compassion for the hurting. Plant in me that same passion.

LENTEN ACTION

Engage in some form of social-justice work this Lent. If possible, participate locally in a Habitat for Humanity project or volunteer with an after-school tutoring program or a homeless or women's shelter. As you do this work, imagine how society might be made more just; as you encounter people who are hurting, make an effort to extend to them dignity as well as compassion.

DAY 7

Old Things New

*I*t is of the new things that men tire—of fashions and pro-
posals and improvements and change. It is the old things
that startle and intoxicate. It is the old things that are young.
There is no skeptic who does not feel that many have doubted
before. There is no rich and fickle man who does not feel that all
his novelties are ancient. There is no worshipper of change who
does not feel upon his neck the vast weight of the weariness of
the universe. But we who do the old things are fed by nature with
a perpetual infancy.

THE NAPOLEON OF NOTTING HILL

ASK FOR THE ANCIENT PATHS

Thus says the LORD:
Stand at the crossroads, and look,
    and ask for the ancient paths,
where the good way lies; and walk in it,
    and find rest for your souls.
But they said, "We will not walk in it."

JEREMIAH 6:16

PRAYER

Lord of the Exodus and of the resurrection, you have guided my steps and smoothed my path. You appeared in my story before I was ever born. Even when I was far away from you—even when I fled from you—you were behind and before me, above and beneath me: protecting, guiding, loving, and nudging me always nearer to you. Thank you for your presence in my past. Teach me to meditate gratefully on your footprints through my history.

LENTEN ACTION

Write or outline the spiritual history of your family. At what points do ancient Christian practices (such as baptism, Eucharist, or pilgrimage) intersect with your family's spiritual history? Can you identify individuals "sent" by God to act as mediators between God and your faith? Thank God for the legacy of faith that has been passed down to you.

The Mind of the Mob

The poor to whom he preached the good news, the common people who heard him gladly, the populace that had made so many popular heroes and demigods in the old pagan world, showed also the weaknesses that were dissolving the world. They suffered the evils often seen in the mob of the city, and especially the mob of the capital, during the decline of a society. The same thing that makes the rural population live on tradition makes the urban population live on rumor....Some brigand or other was artificially turned into a picturesque and popular figure and run as a kind of candidate against Christ. In all this we recognize the urban population that we know, with its newspaper scares and scoops. But there was present in this ancient population an evil more peculiar to the ancient world....It was the soul of the hive; a heathen thing....The mob went along with the Sadducees and the Pharisees, the philosophers and the moralists. It went along with the imperial magistrates and the sacred priests, the scribes and the soldiers, that the one universal human spirit might suffer a universal condemnation; that there might be one deep, unanimous chorus of approval and harmony when Man was rejected of men.

THE EVERLASTING MAN

THE MOB CHOOSES

Now at the festival he used to release a prisoner for them, anyone for whom they asked. Now a man called Barabbas was in prison with the rebels who had committed murder during the insurrection. So the crowd came and began to ask Pilate to do for them according to his custom. Then he answered them, "Do you want me to release for you the King of the Jews?" For he realized that it was out of jealousy that the chief priests had handed him over. But the chief priests stirred up the crowd to have him release Barabbas for them instead. Pilate spoke to them again, "Then what do you wish me to do with the man you call the King of the Jews?" They shouted back, "Crucify him!" Pilate asked them, "Why, what evil has he done?" But they shouted all the more, "Crucify him!" So Pilate, wishing to satisfy the crowd, released Barabbas for them; and after flogging Jesus, he handed him over to be crucified.

MARK 15:6–15

PRAYER

Lord, the world seeps into me like moisture through cracks in basement concrete; it grows as stealthily as creeping vines. I don't even notice how my attitudes are being twisted by external forces. I realize the world is not completely depraved. Culture, custom, art, science, literature, can all serve as conduits of your Spirit. But grant me a discriminating heart so I can recognize when I am taking on attitudes and engaging in actions that would shame me before you.

LENTEN ACTION

Where do you find yourself mindlessly going along with culture? List seven to ten ways you tend to conform to the world. List four ways you can be transformed by being in but not of the world. Circle two that stand out to you as especially practical or feasible. Choose one of those two to work on this Lent.

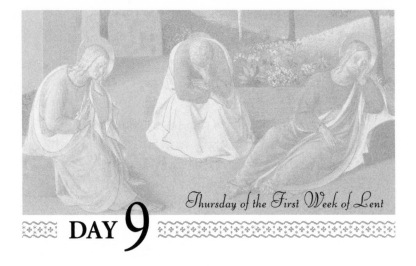

DAY 9

A Double Benefit

ℬecket wore a hair shirt under his gold and crimson, and there is much to be said for the combination; for Becket got the benefit of the hair shirt while the people in the street got the benefit of the crimson and gold. It is at least better than the manner of the modern millionaire, who has the black and the drab outwardly for others, and the gold next [to] his heart.

ORTHODOXY

YOUR FATHER, WHO SEES IN SECRET

> *"And whenever you fast, do not look dismal, like the hypo-crites, for they disfigure their faces so as to show others that they are fasting. Truly I tell you, they have received their reward. But when you fast, put oil on your head and wash your face, so that your fasting may be seen not by others but by your Father who is in secret; and your Father who sees in secret will reward you."*

MATTHEW 6:16–18

PRAYER

Father, you know us in secret, and you know all our secret places. What we do to benefit your kingdom will not be lost if it is not seen by others, for you see and you reward according to your grace and mercy. Strengthen us to do good works, visibly or invisibly, always in your name.

LENTEN ACTION

Today do one thing in secret that you are quite sure would receive the praise of others if they knew of it.

DAY 10

The Cross

*T*he cross cannot be defeated…
for it is Defeat."

MacIan, in *The Ball and the Cross*

BANDITS, CHIEF PRIESTS, AND SCRIBES

It was nine o'clock in the morning when they crucified him.
The inscription of the charge against him read, "The King of
the Jews." And with him they crucified two bandits, one on
his right and one on his left. Those who passed by derided
him, shaking their heads and saying, "Aha! You who would
destroy the temple and build it in three days, save yourself,
and come down from the cross!" In the same way the chief
priests, along with the scribes, were also mocking him among
themselves and saying, "He saved others; he cannot save
himself. Let the Messiah, the King of Israel, come down

from the cross now, so that we may see and believe." Those who were crucified with him also taunted him.

MARK 15:25–32

PRAYER

Lord Jesus, you were mocked by bandits, chief priests, and scribes. Had we been there ourselves, we confess, we may have joined in. Forgive us all who—then and now—understand your mysterious power too poorly. Teach us humility; teach us gratitude.

LENTEN ACTION

As a reminder of Christ's sacrifice and suffering, wear a cross today.

DAY 11

The Sword of Surprise

Sunder me from my bones, O sword of God,
   Till they stand stark and strange as do the trees;
That I whose heart goes up with the soaring woods
May marvel as much at these.

Sunder me from my blood that in the dark
I hear that red ancestral river run,
Like branching buried floods that find the sea
But never see the sun.

Give me miraculous eyes to see my eyes,
Those rolling mirrors made alive in me,
Terrible crystal more incredible
Than all the things they see.

Sunder me from my soul, that I may see
The sins like streaming wounds, the life's brave beat;
Till I shall save myself, as I would save
A stranger in the street.

COLLECTED POETRY

WORD-SWORD SUNDERING

Let us therefore make every effort to enter that rest, so that no one may fall through such disobedience as theirs. Indeed, the word of God is living and active, sharper than any two-edged sword, piercing until it divides soul from spirit, joints from marrow; it is able to judge the thoughts and intentions of the heart. And before him no creature is hidden, but all are naked and laid bare to the eyes of the one to whom we must render an account. Since, then, we have a great high priest who has passed through the heavens, Jesus, the Son of God, let us hold fast to our confession.

HEBREWS 4:11–14

PRAYER

Lord, search me and know me. May the real me learn how to pray honestly to the real you. I don't even know myself—my motivations, my subconscious yearnings. From where do my anxieties spring? Why are my desires sometimes so overpowering but other times so anemic? Show me my cowardice and make me braver. Show me my lusts and make me more chaste. Show me my secret envy and pride and make me more humble. Show me not only what I am in my weakness but what you desire to make me through the power of Christ's cross.

LENTEN ACTION

Sit down with your journal or a piece of paper. Reflect in writing (a rough sketch is enough at first) on the last year of your life, noting some of the main high and low points. Next, draw two parallel horizontal lines across the page. Graph the ups and downs you have recently experienced. Can you interpret these observations you have made? Meditate on the exercise, asking God to show you what God wants you to perceive through it. Is it possible for you to discern God's presence in the low points as well as in the high points?

DAY 12

Hospitality

Comfort is not always a contemptible thing, when its other name is hospitality.

ROBERT LOUIS STEVENSON

GOOD STEWARDS

Be hospitable to one another without complaining. Like good stewards of the manifold grace of God, serve one another with whatever gift each of you has received.

1 PETER 4:9–10

PRAYER

God of Manifold Grace, Giver of Manifold Gifts, help us to be as generous with the gifts you have given us as you were when you first gave them to us. Protect us from stinginess, from complaining. Teach us to love as you love.

LENTEN ACTION

In your dealings with others today, try to push yourself to the point of complaining. When you sense that you have given of yourself almost more than you care to, pause and say a brief prayer asking God for the strength to give more or the wisdom to rest a while.

DAY 13

Thread of Thanks

I invented a rudimentary and makeshift mystical theory of my own. It was substantially this; that even mere existence, reduced to its most primary limits, was extraordinary enough to be exciting. Anything was magnificent as compared with nothing. Even if the very daylight were a dream, it was a day-dream; it was not a nightmare. The mere fact that one could wave one's arms and legs about...showed that it had not the mere paralysis of a nightmare. Or if it was a nightmare, it was an enjoyable nightmare....[N]o man knows how much he is an optimist, even when he calls himself a pessimist, because he has not really measured the depths of his debt to whatever created him and enabled him to call himself anything. At the back of our brains, so to speak, there was a forgotten blaze or burst of astonishment at our own existence. The object of the artistic and spiritual life was to dig for this submerged sunrise of wonder; so that a man sitting in a chair might suddenly understand that he was actually alive, and be happy.

THE AUTOBIOGRAPHY

SATISFIED WITH THE GOOD

Bless the LORD, O my soul,
and all that is within me,
bless his holy name.
Bless the LORD, O my soul,
and do not forget all his benefits—
who forgives all your iniquity,
who heals all your diseases,
who redeems your life from the Pit,
who crowns you with steadfast love and mercy,
who satisfies you with good as long as you live
so that your youth is renewed like the eagle's.

PSALM 103:1–5

PRAYER

Lord, I confess that too often I see the glass as half empty instead of half full. I see problems instead of potential, obstacles instead of opportunities. Give me eyes to see the miracle of life within me and all around me. Give me eyes to perceive the grace of every human face, to marvel at the movement of my limbs, to wonder at the wind. This day, Lord, let me be amazed at this precious gift of life you have loaned me.

LENTEN ACTION

In your journal or on a piece of paper, draw a line down the middle of a page, splitting the page into two columns. On the left side, make a list of things for which you are grateful. As God brings new blessings to your mind during the week, add to your list. In the right-hand column, comment on these blessings, recording your thoughts of amazement, wonder, and joy.

DAY 14

The Riddles of God

*T*his, I say, is the first fact touching the speech; the fine inspiration by which God comes in at the end, not to answer riddles, but to propound them. The other great fact which, taken together with this one, makes the whole work religious instead of merely philosophical is that other great surprise which makes Job suddenly satisfied with the mere presentation of something impenetrable. Verbally speaking the enigmas of Jehovah seem darker and more desolate than the enigmas of Job; yet Job was comfortless before the speech of Jehovah and is comforted after it. He has been told nothing, but he feels the terrible and tingling atmosphere of something which is too good to be told. The refusal of God to explain His design is itself a burning hint of His design. The riddles of God are more satisfying than the solutions of man.

"INTRODUCTION TO THE BOOK OF JOB," *G. K. C. AS M. C.*

OUT OF THE WHIRLWIND

Then the LORD answered Job out of the whirlwind:
"Who is this that darkens counsel by words without
knowledge?
Gird up your loins like a man,
I will question you, and you shall declare to me.

"Where were you when I laid the foundation of the earth?
Tell me, if you have understanding.
Who determined its measurements—surely you know!
Or who stretched the line upon it?
On what were its bases sunk,
or who laid its cornerstone
when the morning stars sang together
and all the heavenly beings shouted for joy?"

JOB 38:1–7

PRAYER

God almighty, maker of heaven and earth, have mercy on me for my lack of faith, for too easily grumbling and grousing about your governance of the universe. Sometimes the injustice, the cruelty, and the insanity of our world overwhelms me—and I freeze. Grant me an obedient heart more willing to submit to you, more willing to offer myself in significant ways as part of the solution to my own prayers.

LENTEN ACTION

Take a walk or hike today. Try to peer into the depth and intricacy of the created order. Admit in prayer all the things you cannot fathom. Humble yourself, thanking God for the mystery of the universe.

DAY 15

The Wrong Road

*F*or it is often necessary to walk backwards, as a man on the wrong road goes back to a signpost to find the right road. The modern man is more like a traveler who has forgotten the name of his destination, and has to go back whence he came, even to find out where he is going.

THE NEW JERUSALEM

A SON RETURNS

"I will get up and go to my father, and I will say to him, 'Father, I have sinned against heaven and before you; I am no longer worthy to be called your son.'"

LUKE 15:18–19

PRAYER

Merciful Father, have mercy on us when we do not follow in your light. Bring us quickly back to you. Remind us that in you we have a good father who loves us and will deal graciously with us.

LENTEN ACTION

Lent is a time to examine our lives and to see the sins that we've hidden from ourselves. Like the prodigal son, we should recall who we are—God's own children—and waste no time in returning. In your prayers today, ask God to reveal your sins to you. Ask for God's help in acknowledging these and removing them from your life.

DAY 16

A Perfect Play, Ruined

*A*ccording to most philosophers, God in making the world enslaved it. According to Christianity, in making it, He set it free. God had written, not so much a poem, but rather a play; a play he had planned as perfect, but which had necessarily been left to human actors and stage-managers, who had since made a great mess of it.

ORTHODOXY

ALIVE IN CHRIST

> *For since death came through a human being, the resurrection of the dead has also come through a human being; for as all die in Adam, so all will be made alive in Christ.*

1 CORINTHIANS 15:21–22

PRAYER

Gracious Father, you made this world and you made us. Through us, death entered the world and stayed. By our own efforts, we could not bring life back again, and so you, in your mercy, sent your Son to become human and to do what no human could. In him we are made alive. And for this we give you all our thanks.

LENTEN ACTION

Over the years, several movies have been made to retell parts of the biblical story. Choose one of these to watch sometime this week. As you watch the movie, consider how Chesterton's analogy of the world to a play illuminates your understanding.

DAY 17

Prefigured Wounds

The book of Job is chiefly remarkable, as I have insisted throughout, for the fact that it does not end in a way that is conventionally satisfactory. Job is not told that his misfortunes were due to his sins or a part of any plan for his improvement. But in the prologue we see Job tormented not because he was the worst of men, but because he was the best. It is the lesson of the whole work that man is most comforted by paradoxes. Here is the very darkest and strangest of the paradoxes; and it is by all human testimony the most reassuring. I need not suggest what high and strange history awaited this paradox of the best man in the worst fortune. I need not say that in the freest and most philosophical sense there is one Old Testament figure who is truly a type; or say what is prefigured in the wounds of Job.

"INTRODUCTION TO THE BOOK OF JOB," *G. K. C. AS M. C.*

MY REDEEMER LIVES

For I know that my Redeemer lives,
  and that at the last he will stand upon the earth;
and after my skin has been thus destroyed,
  then in my flesh I shall see God,
whom I shall see on my side,
  and my eyes shall behold, and not another.
My heart faints within me!

JOB 19:25–27

PRAYER

Lord, you who have been wounded, forgive me; for so often I live only for myself. My life revolves around my little world of what I want and what I fear. May my agenda decrease while joy for your agenda matures in me. Grow in me a spiritually attentive, larger, more generous heart. Help me redirect myself and my concerns outwardly toward your Spirit, who dwells in the people around me.

LENTEN ACTION

This week visit someone who is suffering: someone grieving, someone who lies sick or in the hospital, someone experiencing loneliness or depression. Concentrate on listening to their story. After you "break the ice" with a few good questions, try not to speak unnecessarily. Instead, listen to their pain and empathize with their situation. Before leaving, offer to pray for them. As you do, can you imagine the crucified Christ suffering with them?

DAY 18 — *Saturday of the Second Week of Lent*

Influencing Children

*A*young mother remarked to me, "I don't want to teach my child any religion. I don't want to influence him; I want him to choose for himself when he grows up." That is a very ordinary example of current argument, which is frequently repeated and yet never really applied. Of course the mother was always influencing the child. Of course the mother might just as well have said, "I hope he will choose his own friends when he grows up; so I won't introduce him to any aunts or uncles."

GENERALLY SPEAKING

WISE AND GLAD HEARTS

My child, if your heart is wise,
my heart too will be glad.
My soul will rejoice
when your lips speak what is right.

PROVERBS 23:15–16

PRAYER

Instruct us, Heavenly Father, through your Scripture and through your saints, how to live in wisdom and righteousness. Guide us when we try to instruct those whom you have given us to care for. Let us be lights for your sake.

LENTEN ACTION

Sometimes humility causes us to question the influence we might have over others. At such times it is difficult to know whether to speak or be silent. And yet at that very moment, the Holy Spirit might be urging us to action. If you find yourself in this circumstance today, pause and say a brief prayer asking God to guide your behavior.

DAY 19

Like an Exuberant Tree

*I*t is in our own daily life that we are to look for the portents and the prodigies....Compared with this life, all public life, all fame, all wisdom, is by its nature cramped and cold and small. For on that defined and lighted public stage men are of necessity forced to profess one set of accomplishments, to rise to one rigid standard. It is the utterly unknown people, who can grow in all directions like an exuberant tree.

CHARLES DICKENS

HELD OF NO ACCOUNT

Who has believed what we have heard?
*   And to whom has the arm of the LORD been revealed?*
For he grew up before him like a young plant,
*   and like a root out of dry ground;*
he had no form or majesty that we should look at him,
*   nothing in his appearance that we should desire him.*

He was despised and rejected by others;
a man of suffering and acquainted with infirmity;
and as one from whom others hide their faces
he was despised, and we held him of no account.

ISAIAH 53:1–3

PRAYER

Lord Christ, you chose lowliness rather than grandeur; you served others, though you are the most worthy to be served. Teach us the example of your meekness. Let us not be distracted by false appearances and false claims to power. May we, like you, care more for others than for ourselves, and may we care more for your opinion of us than what others may think.

LENTEN ACTION

Often we are judged favorably or unfavorably based on our appearance. For today, alter your appearance in a way that lessens your desirability but doesn't call undue attention to you. You might, for instance, wear less fashionable clothes or spend less time on your grooming. The aim of this exercise is modesty.

Love of Limits

It is plain on the face of the facts that the child is positively in love with limits. He uses his imagination to invent imaginary limits. The nurse and the governess have never told him that it is his moral duty to step on alternative paving-stones. He deliberately deprives this world of half its paving-stones, in order to exult in a challenge that he has offered to himself....This game of self-limitation is one of the secret pleasures of life. As it says in the little manuals about such sports, the game is played in several forms. One very good way of playing it is to look at the nearest bookcase and wonder whether you would find sufficient entertainment in that chance collection, even if you had no other books. But always it is dominated by this principle of division and restriction, which begins with the game played by the child with the paving-stones....If anybody chooses to say that I have founded all my social philosophy on the antics of a baby, I am quite satisfied to bow and smile.

"ON THE ROMANCE OF CHILDHOOD," *ALL IS GRIST*

KEEP MY STEPS

Your decrees are wonderful;
 therefore my soul keeps them.
The unfolding of your words gives light;
 it imparts understanding to the simple.
With open mouth I pant,
 because I long for your commandments.
Turn to me and be gracious to me,
 as is your custom toward those who love your name.
Keep my steps steady according to your promise,
 and never let iniquity have dominion over me.
Redeem me from human oppression,
 that I may keep your precepts.
Make your face shine upon your servant,
 and teach me your statutes.

PSALM 119:129–135

PRAYER

Lord, giver of all good gifts, lend me eyes to see the wonder of life. Some of the most beautiful things in life are the most simple and most common—a sunset, a smile, good sauerkraut. Fill me with grace, that I might appreciate the things I have: the world around me, family and friends, your purpose for my life. Grant me wisdom to set for myself healthy limits. And let those limits set me free—free to enjoy what is instead of fettered over what might or might not be.

LENTEN ACTION

During Lent we often speak of fasting. Rather than focusing merely on food, fast from something else this week. Consider what is driving you lately. If you are hurried, perhaps fast from speeding. If you have been a couch potato, why not unplug for a week? If through this fasting you end up with more free time, try to spend it in prayer, in relationships, or simply in the renewal that comes from resting.

DAY 21

Who Can Be Humble?

*A god can be humble,
a devil can only be humbled."*

MACIAN, IN *THE BALL AND THE CROSS*

HE HUMBLED HIMSELF

*[Jesus], though he was in the form of God,
    did not regard equality with God
    as something to be exploited,
but emptied himself,
    taking the form of a slave,
    being born in human likeness.
And being found in human form,
    he humbled himself
    and became obedient to the point of death—
    even death on a cross.*

PHILIPPIANS 2:6–8

[Jesus] said to them, "I watched Satan fall from heaven like a flash of lightning."

LUKE 10:18

PRAYER

Gracious Father, help us to be humble. May we not misuse the power or status we have, seeing that Christ, equal to you, did not do so. We pray earnestly that we might follow his example and humble ourselves.

LENTEN ACTION

Without calling undue attention to your actions, humble yourself today. Serve someone whose job it is to serve you. Freely relinquish the power you have over an "inferior" and reflect how truly inferior you are to Christ, who nevertheless made himself your servant of grace.

DAY 22

Washing Windows

The weakness of pride lies after all in this; that oneself is a window. It can be a colored window, if you will; but the more thickly you lay on the colors the less of a window it will be. The two things to be done with a window are to wash it and then forget it. So the truly pious have always said the two things to do personally are to cleanse and to forget oneself.

"MATTHEW ARNOLD," *G. K. C. AS M. C.*

CONFESS AND BE FORGIVEN

If we say that we have no sin, we deceive ourselves, and the truth is not in us. If we confess our sins, he who is faithful and just will forgive us our sins and cleanse us from all unrighteousness.

1 JOHN 1:8–9

PRAYER

Undeceive us, Faithful One, that knowing the truth, we may confess it to you. We trust in your justice and mercy. We long for your forgiveness.

LENTEN ACTION

As a way to remind yourself of the importance of confessing our sins and being forgiven, pay a little closer attention to the windows you see today. Let them stand for you, as they did for Chesterton, as a symbol of how we should care for ourselves—"wash...and then forget."

DAY 23

Playing at Life

$\mathcal{I}$t might reasonably be maintained that the true object of all human life is play. Earth is a task garden; heaven is a playground. To be at last in such secure innocence that one can juggle with the universe and the stars, to be so good that one can treat everything as a joke—that may be, perhaps, the real end and final holiday of human souls.

"ARISTOCRACY AT OUR UNIVERSITIES,"
ILLUSTRATED LONDON NEWS, AUGUST 17, 1907

POWER TO BECOME CHILDREN OF GOD

He was in the world, and the world came into being through him; yet the world did not know him. He came to what was his own, and his own people did not accept him. But to all who received him, who believed in his name, he gave power to become children of God.

JOHN 1:10–12

PRAYER

God almighty, maker of monkeys, giver of giraffes, forgive us for taking ourselves too seriously, for our false grownup-ness, which feigns adult maturity merely as a guise to dominate others. Replant in us, O God, seeds of simple faith, the power to become your children, and reset in us eyes of wonder and innocence to experience the world again as your merry playground.

LENTEN ACTION

Set aside at least an hour today for "holy play." In his autobiography Chesterton spoke of devoting serious time to "solid and constructive work like cutting out cardboard figures and pasting colored tinsel upon them." If appropriate, include either children or a pet in your merriment. If not, conceive of some enjoyable activity and carry it out as an act of praise. As you begin, invite God not only to make your play sacramental but also to join in the festivities with you.

The Best of the World at Its Worst

All the great groups that stood about the Cross represent in one way or another the great historical truth of the time; that the world could not save itself. Man could do no more. Rome and Jerusalem and Athens and everything else were going down like a sea turned into a slow cataract. Externally indeed the ancient world was still at its strongest; it is always at that moment that the inmost weakness begins. But in order to understand that weakness we must repeat what has been said more than once; that it was not the weakness of a thing originally weak. It was emphatically the strength of the world that was turned to weakness and the wisdom of the world that was turned to folly.

In this story of Good Friday it is the best things in the world that are at their worst. That is what really shows us the world at its worst. It was, for instance, the priests of a true monotheism and the soldiers of an international civilization. Rome, the legend, founded upon fallen Troy and triumphant over fallen Carthage, had stood for a heroism which was the nearest that any pagan ever came to chivalry....Skepticism has eaten away even the confident sanity of the conquerors of the world. He who is enthroned to say what is justice can only ask: "What is truth?"

THE EVERLASTING MAN

WHAT IS TRUTH?

Then Pilate entered the headquarters again, summoned Jesus, and asked him, "Are you the King of the Jews?" Jesus answered, "Do you ask this on your own, or did others tell you about me?" Pilate replied, "I am not a Jew, am I? Your own nation and the chief priests have handed you over to me. What have you done?" Jesus answered, "My kingdom is not from this world. If my kingdom were from this world, my followers would be fighting to keep me from being handed over to the Jews. But as it is, my kingdom is not from here." Pilate asked him, "So you are a king?" Jesus answered, "You say that I am a king. For this I was born, and for this I came into the world, to testify to the truth. Everyone who belongs to the truth listens to my voice." Pilate asked him, "What is truth?"

JOHN 18:33–38

PRAYER

Lord, as I examine my conscience, I am prone either to dismiss my sin too easily or to trust too little in your forgiveness. To which of these errors am I most susceptible right now, Holy God? Teach me, Gracious Shepherd, to practice my confession regularly—not from fear, nor merely from drear habit, but with the same solemn, sacramental joy of a lover apologizing to his or her beloved.

LENTEN ACTION

In your journal or on a piece of paper, draw a line down the middle of a page. On the left side, make a list of what you consider your strengths. Then make notes in the right-hand column on where your strengths tend to become weaknesses. Does your love become possessiveness; your thrift, miserliness; your friendship, gossip; or your leadership, manipulation? Vow to pay more attention to your "shadow" side, asking God for healing and trust.

DAY 25

Outside All of Us

When we belong to the Church we belong to something which is outside all of us; which is outside everything you talk about, outside the Cardinals and the Pope. They belong to it, but it does not belong to them. If we all fell dead suddenly, the Church would still somehow exist in God."

MACIAN, IN *THE BALL AND THE CROSS*

ONE BODY

For as in one body we have many members, and not all the members have the same function, so we, who are many, are one body in Christ, and individually we are members one of another. We have gifts that differ according to the grace given to us: prophecy, in proportion to faith; ministry, in ministering; the teacher, in teaching; the exhorter, in exhortation; the giver, in generosity; the leader, in diligence; the compassionate, in cheerfulness.

ROMANS 12:4–8

PRAYER

Heavenly Father, through your Holy Spirit, we are one body. Teach us to value this unity. When we are not sure what our gifts are, show us, we pray, that we may do our work as living members of your church.

LENTEN ACTION

Dedicate part of today to a "gift hunt." When you notice in a family member, a friend, a coworker, or a companion one of the gifts listed in today's passage from Romans, point it out. Depending on the situation, you may want to make a silent note of the gift. Other times it may seem best to tell the person that he or she is generous or cheerful or a good teacher. We often learn our gifts best when others point them out to us.

DAY 26

Turn Your Cheek

*I*t is true that we cannot turn the cheek to the smiter; it is true that we cannot give our cloak to the robber; civilization is too complicated, too vainglorious, too emotional....The command of Christ is impossible, but it is not insane; it is rather sanity preached to a planet of lunatics. If the whole world was suddenly stricken with a sense of humor it would find itself mechanically fulfilling the Sermon on the Mount. It is not the plain facts of the world which stand in the way of that consummation, but its passions of vanity and self-advertisement and morbid sensibility. It is true that we cannot turn the cheek to the smiter, and the sole and sufficient reason is that we have not the pluck.

TWELVE TYPES

THE MIND OF THE MAKER

If then there is any encouragement in Christ, any consolation from love, any sharing in the Spirit, any compassion and sympathy, make my joy complete: be of the same mind,

*having the same love, being in full accord and of one mind.
Do nothing from selfish ambition or conceit, but in humility
regard others as better than yourselves. Let each of you look
not to your own interests, but to the interests of others. Let
the same mind be in you that was in Christ Jesus.*

PHILIPPIANS 2:1–5

PRAYER

Lord, I confess that it is all too easy for me to blame, criticize, gossip, snub, and pout. Much of this misbehavior is rooted in envy or fear, in low self-esteem or lack of faith. Help me see not only my sin but a purer way in Christ, a way of love rooted in you. Help me take steps to practice forgiveness.

LENTEN ACTION

In your journal or on a piece of paper, draw a diagram that represents the various people in your life—at home, school, or work—on a hypothetical ladder of power. Where do you fit in this configuration? Name the key people in your life with whom you struggle for power. Determine today to grant dignity and a voice to those people below you on the ladder, and pray for any above you on the ladder as you encounter them. Make an effort to say nothing this week that advances your own self-image.

DAY 27

The Loud Soup and the Chatty Asparagus

*S*ometimes a guest is actually described as being invited to a "quiet dinner." It is rather a quaint phrase when one considers it; as implying that the dinner itself could be noisy; that the soup would roar like the sea, or the asparagus become talkative, or the mutton-chop shriek aloud like the mandrake. But it does bear witness to the normal conception of comfort; that a quiet dinner means a quiet talk.

"ON THE PRISON OF JAZZ," *AVOWALS AND DENIALS*

BREAKFAST WITH THE LORD

When they [the disciples] had gone ashore, they saw a charcoal fire there, with fish on it, and bread. Jesus said to them, "Bring some of the fish that you have just caught.... Come and have breakfast." Now none of the disciples dared to ask him, "Who are you?" because they knew it was the Lord. Jesus came and took the bread and gave it to them, and did the same with the fish. This was now the third time that Jesus appeared to the disciples after he was raised from the dead.

JOHN 21:9–10, 12–14

PRAYER

Lord Jesus, Risen Christ, you fed your disciples and you feed us too. As we break bread, remind us that you are here with us, that we are all one in your mystical body.

LENTEN ACTION

Invite a friend to have a "quiet dinner" with you this week. Let your conversation be the centerpiece that the food surrounds.

DAY 28

Not Labor but Leisure

*W*hen two business men in a train are talking about dollars, I am not so foolish as to expect them to be talking about the philosophy of St. Thomas Aquinas. But if they were two English business men I should not expect them to be talking about business. Probably it would be about some sport; and most probably some sport in which they themselves never dreamed of indulging. The approximate difference is that the American talks about his work and the Englishman about his holidays. His ideal is not labor but leisure.

WHAT I SAW IN AMERICA

RETURN TO YOUR REST

The LORD protects the simple;
when I was brought low, he saved me.
Return, O my soul, to your rest,
for the LORD has dealt bountifully with you.

PSALM 116:6–7

PRAYER

Our bodies, Lord, grow weak. Our spirits and our minds tire even when we don't know it. We need our Sabbaths. Help us to remember to rest. Interrupt our constant thoughts of business and activity, that we might refresh our minds, spirits, and bodies.

LENTEN ACTION

Plan for a thirty-minute recess today. Before you begin your work or activity, schedule a time to relax in a quiet setting. When you are there, say to yourself the second verse of the psalm quoted today.

The Logic of Charity

"People who lose all their charity generally lose all their logic."

FATHER BROWN, IN *THE FATHER BROWN OMNIBUS*

PROCLAIMING MERCY

They came to Jesus and saw the demoniac sitting there, clothed and in his right mind, the very man who had had the legion; and they were afraid. Those who had seen what had happened to the demoniac and to the swine reported it. Then they began to beg Jesus to leave their neighborhood. As he was getting into the boat, the man who had been possessed by demons begged him that he might be with him. But Jesus refused, and said to him, "Go home to your friends, and tell them how much the Lord has done for you, and what mercy he has shown you." And he went away and began to proclaim in the Decapolis how much Jesus had done for him; and everyone was amazed.

MARK 5:15–20

PRAYER

Through your death on the cross, Lord Jesus, you have shown all of us your mercy. Thank you for your unfathomable love. Help us as we proclaim this great good news to the world.

LENTEN ACTION

Chart the rise and fall of your charity today. Make a mental note of the times when you feel the least charitable toward another, and then consider today's brief quote from Chesterton. Did your loss of charity coincide with an equal loss of logic? Were you being in some way unreasonable when you ran out of charity?

DAY 30

Turning Hate to Love

hese are the things which might conceivably and truly make men forgive their enemies. We can only turn hate to love by understanding what are the things that men have loved; nor is it necessary to ask men to hate their loves in order to love one another.

And just as two grocers are most likely to be reconciled when they remember for a moment that they are two fathers, so two nationals are most likely to be reconciled when they remember (if only for a moment) that they are two patriots.

"THE INTRINSIC VALUE OF THE NATION,"
ILLUSTRATED LONDON NEWS, JUNE 4, 1921

EYE FOR AN EYE

"You have heard that it was said, 'An eye for an eye and a tooth for a tooth.' But I say to you, Do not resist an evildoer. But if anyone strikes you on the right cheek, turn the other also; and if anyone wants to sue you and take your coat,

give your cloak as well; and if anyone forces you to go one mile, go also the second mile. Give to everyone who begs from you, and do not refuse anyone who wants to borrow from you."

MATTHEW 5:38–42

PRAYER

Who am I, God, that I should consider myself superior to others—worth special treatment or consideration? Open my heart to understand my fellow men and women, especially those with whom I currently experience conflict. Open my mind to comprehend that I am connected to other human beings; that my sense of individual separateness is in reality an illusion. Teach me, Lord, first to understand my enemies and then even to love them.

LENTEN ACTION

Spend ten to twenty minutes in silent prayer. As distractions crowd your mind, do not hold on to them; let them go. After you find some soul silence, ask God to bring to your mind your "enemies." Imagine, as Chesterton suggests above, ways you are alike. Ask God what you have in common with these people. Finally, ask God to show you ways you might take small steps toward reconciliation—a card or phone call, a smile or handshake.

The King Among Us

*N*othing short of the extreme and strong and startling doctrine of the divinity of Christ will give that particular effect that can truly stir the popular sense like a trumpet; the idea of the king himself serving in the ranks like a common soldier. By making that figure merely human we make that story much less human. We take away the point of the story which actually pierces humanity; the point of the story which was quite literally the point of a spear. It does not especially humanize the universe to say that good and wise men can die for their opinions; any more than it would be any sort of uproariously popular news in an army that good soldiers may easily get killed.

THE EVERLASTING MAN

THE FIRSTBORN OF ALL CREATION

He is the image of the invisible God, the firstborn of all creation; for in him all things in heaven and on earth were created, things visible and invisible, whether thrones

*or dominions or rulers or powers—all things have been
created through him and for him. He himself is before all
things, and in him all things hold together. He is the head
of the body, the church; he is the beginning, the firstborn
from the dead, so that he might come to have first place in
everything. For in him all the fullness of God was pleased
to dwell, and through him God was pleased to reconcile to
himself all things, whether on earth or in heaven, by making
peace through the blood of his cross.*

COLOSSIANS 1:15–20

PRAYER

Lord, I cannot truly fathom the complete coexistence of
your human and divine natures in one person. Even less
can I fathom your humility, which condescended to put
on my humanity. I stand in awe of your amazing love—
that the King of Glory should bleed and die for me. Accept
this imperfect gratitude that I offer you, dear Lord, as a
wise and loving parent receives gifts from a child.

LENTEN ACTION

Do a study of paintings of Jesus. Notice which ones emphasize his humanity and which ones tend to emphasize
his divinity. List in your journal or on a piece of paper the
ways artists depict Christ's deity. Use some images you
glean from this exercise in meditative prayer today.

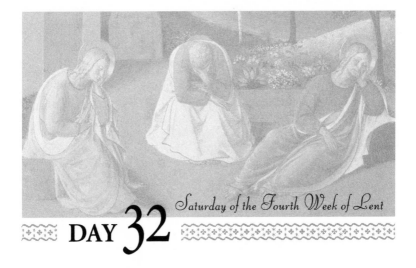

DAY 32

Happiness Doubled by Wonder

I would maintain that thanks are the highest form of thought;
and that gratitude is happiness doubled by wonder.

A Short History of England

THANKS BE TO GOD

*But thanks be to God, who gives us the victory through our
Lord Jesus Christ.*

1 Corinthians 15:57

PRAYER

Father of Our Lord Jesus Christ, thank you for caring for
us beyond our ability to comprehend. We wonder at such
love that would sacrifice all for us—God who humbles
himself, becomes a man, and dies to bring life. Let our
astounded thanks and our faithful service to your will be
our small payment—never enough but all that we have.

LENTEN ACTION

Consider today's Scripture quote from First Corinthians. Through Jesus Christ we are all promised a victory over death. What other victories have come to you through believing in and following Jesus? Make a mental list or write one on paper. Thank God for each of these victories that come through knowing God's Son.

DAY 33

A Wind of Everlasting Life

*I*n every century, in this century, in the next century, the Passion is what it was in the first century, when it occurred; a thing stared at by a crowd. It remains a tragedy of the people; a crime of the people; a consolation of the people; but never merely a thing of the period....It lives, because it involves the staggering story of the Creator truly groaning and travailing with his Creation; and the highest thing thinkable passing through some nadir of the lowest curve of the cosmos. And it lives, because the very blast from this black cloud of death comes upon the world as a wind of everlasting life; by which all things wake and are alive.

THE WAY OF THE CROSS

JESUS, THE PIONEER OF FAITH

Therefore, since we are surrounded by so great a cloud of witnesses, let us also lay aside every weight and the sin that clings so closely, and let us run with perseverance the race that is set before us, looking to Jesus the pioneer and perfecter of our faith, who for the sake of the joy that was set before him endured the cross, disregarding its shame, and has taken his seat at the right hand of the throne of God. Consider him who endured such hostility against himself from sinners, so that you may not grow weary or lose heart. In your struggle against sin you have not yet resisted to the point of shedding your blood.

HEBREWS 12:1–4

PRAYER

God, wake me. Merciful Lord, shake me. Father, show me the depths of what you have done on the cross. Create in me not only gratitude but a new resolve to lay aside every choking burden and festering sin, that I might follow Christ through the Way of the Cross to a purer, higher humanity in him.

LENTEN ACTION

Find a cross or crucifix to contemplate this week. It can be in picture or statue form. Set aside your cognitive tendencies at this point and open yourself to what God has to tell you personally through this meditation.

DAY 34

Like the World

*O*f course the family is a good institution because it is uncongenial. It is wholesome precisely because it contains so many divergences and varieties. It is…like a little kingdom, and, like most other little kingdoms, is generally in a state of something resembling anarchy.…Aunt Elizabeth is unreasonable, like mankind. Papa is excitable, like mankind. Our youngest brother is mischievous, like mankind. Grandpapa is stupid, like the world; he is old, like the world.

HERETICS

LOVE THE FATHER

Do not love the world or the things in the world. The love of the Father is not in those who love the world; for all that is in the world—the desire of the flesh, the desire of the eyes, the pride in riches—comes not from the Father but from

the world. And the world and its desire are passing away,
but those who do the will of God live forever.

1 JOHN 2:15–17

PRAYER

Continue to teach us, dear God, how to love you and not
the world. We pray that you will reveal our faulty love and
replace it with a true one. And may this love, the love of
you, give us a desire to do your will.

LENTEN ACTION

If you are around family members this week and feel
annoyed by one or more of them, call to mind today's
passage by Chesterton. Try to view your family in a comic
light. If that strategy fails (and it may), remember to pray
for patience and understanding.

:::: **DAY** 35 :::::::::::::::::::::::::::::::

American Idols

*I*dolatry exists wherever the thing which originally gave us happiness becomes at last more important than happiness itself. Drunkenness, for example, may be fairly described as an engrossing hobby. And drunkenness is, when really comprehended in its inward and psychological reality, a typical example of idolatry. Essential intemperance begins at the point where the one incidental form of pleasure, which comes from a certain article of consumption, becomes more important than all the vast universe of natural pleasures, which it finally destroys.

LUNACY AND LETTERS

HAVE YOU NOT UNDERSTOOD?

> *To whom then will you liken God,*
> *   or what likeness compare with him?*
> *An idol?—A workman casts it,*
> *   and a goldsmith overlays it with gold,*
> *   and casts for it silver chains.*

As a gift one chooses mulberry wood
—wood that will not rot—
then seeks out a skilled artisan
to set up an image that will not topple.

Have you not known? Have you not heard?
Has it not been told you from the beginning?
Have you not understood from the foundations of the
earth?
It is he who sits above the circle of the earth,
and its inhabitants are like grasshoppers;
who stretches out the heavens like a curtain,
and spreads them like a tent to live in;
who brings princes to naught,
and makes the rulers of the earth as nothing.

ISAIAH 40:18–23

PRAYER

Lord, my idols are all dead things. They are not living; they cannot act. How do I forget that so easily? Yet they promise to comfort me, Father, when I am afraid, lonely, or dejected, because I can see them. I cannot see you, God, and so I easily lose faith. I instinctively turn to something tangible. O Lord, have mercy on me. I believe; help my unbelief.

LENTEN ACTION

Spend a few minutes in meditation identifying your current idols. Which of these idols could you symbolically confront this week by giving something up, giving something away, or fasting from something for a few days?

DAY 36

Everlastingly Alive

he physical fact of death, in a hundred horrid shapes, was more naked and less veiled in times of faith or superstition than in times of science or skepticism. Often it was not merely those who had seen a man die, but those who had seen him rot, who were most certain that he was everlastingly alive.

FANCIES VERSUS FADS

THE DEAD MAN CAME OUT

Then Jesus, again greatly disturbed, came to the tomb. It was a cave, and a stone was lying against it. Jesus said, "Take away the stone." Martha, the sister of the dead man, said to him, "Lord, already there is a stench because he has been dead four days." Jesus said to her, "Did I not tell you that if you believed, you would see the glory of God?" So they took away the stone. And Jesus looked upward and said, "Father, I thank you for having heard me. I knew that you always hear me, but I have said this for the sake of the crowd stand-

ing here, so that they may believe that you sent me." When he had said this, he cried with a loud voice, "Lazarus, come out!" The dead man came out, his hands and feet bound with strips of cloth, and his face wrapped in a cloth. Jesus said to them, "Unbind him, and let him go."

JOHN 11:38–44

PRAYER

Almighty Father, we give you thanks that you alone hold the power of life, and death, and resurrection. May we do your will in this life, not fearing death nor forgetting the hope of everlasting life, through your Son, our Lord Jesus Christ.

LENTEN ACTION

Choose one of the following exercises as a way to remind yourself of the inevitability of death and the hope of resurrection: (1) read through the obituary page of your local newspaper, pausing to pray for those who have lost a loved one; (2) take a walk in a cemetery and notice the signs of life that surround it—grass, trees, yourself, other visitors; (3) call to mind the names of people you knew who have died, and remember the last words from the Chesterton passage for today, that those individuals are "everlastingly alive."

DAY 37

Respectable Evil

Mr. Kennedy [the playwright] supposes Him [Christ] to be trying to save the reputable people, which is a much larger affair. The chief characters in [the play]…are a popular and strenuous vicar, universally respected, and his fashionable and forcible wife. It would have been no good to tell these people they had some good in them—for that was what they were telling themselves all day long. They had to be reminded that they had some bad in them—instinctive idolatries and silent treasons which they always tried to forget. It is in connection with these crimes of wealth and culture that we face the real problem of positive evil.

A MISCELLANY OF MEN

SOME WHO TRUSTED IN THEMSELVES

He also told this parable to some who trusted in themselves that they were righteous and regarded others with contempt: "Two men went up to the temple to pray, one a Pharisee and the other a tax collector. The Pharisee, standing by himself, was praying thus, 'God, I thank you that I am not like other people: thieves, rogues, adulterers, or even like this tax collector. I fast twice a week; I give a tenth of all my income.' But the tax collector, standing far off, would not even look up to heaven, but was beating his breast and saying, 'God, be merciful to me, a sinner!' I tell you, this man went down to his home justified rather than the other; for all who exalt themselves will be humbled, but all who humble themselves will be exalted."

LUKE 18:9–14

PRAYER

Lord, it is not difficult for me to admit the wickedness of my evil, but it is terribly difficult for me to admit the wickedness of my goodness. If I manage to perform any good deed, I feel superior about it—as though I deserve the credit. I want others to notice, to celebrate me. Teach me humility, Lord: a true and healthy perspective of where I fit in the larger scheme of your work in the world. Help me learn how to give you the credit without falling into trite or simpering platitudes. Grant me the gift of sincerity, Lord.

LENTEN ACTION

Think of an act of kindness you could do anonymously this week. Give a donation or gift anonymously or do some act of service or kindness without taking credit.

Morbid Modernity

*T*here are any number of people now who would say, sincerely if superficially, that it is morbid to stand at all under the Stations of the Cross. As I have noted, they are not altogether consistent. While accusing their fathers of being morbid about faith, they have not even rebuked their contemporaries for being much more morbid about doubt. They have tolerated modern literature which is even darker with defeat and despair; on condition that it contains nothing but defeat and despair.

THE WAY OF THE CROSS

MIXED WITH GALL

After mocking him, they stripped him of the robe and put his own clothes on him. Then they led him away to crucify him. As they went out, they came upon a man from Cyrene named Simon; they compelled this man to carry his cross. And when they came to a place called Golgotha (which means Place of a Skull), they offered him wine to drink, mixed with gall; but when he tasted it, he would not drink it.

MATTHEW 27:31–34

PRAYER

Lord, it is so easy for me to get discouraged. I see obstacles, failures, broken relationships, and a sin-sick world around me. But you took upon yourself all our bent human darkness through your passion and crucifixion. Encourage me to comprehend that ultimately you have defeated darkness, Lord. Grant me more hope, I pray— and faith, and love.

LENTEN ACTION

Contemplatively practice the Stations of the Cross this coming week. If you can find them in a local church— great! If not, locate an art book that depicts them or look online for an artist's rendering. Pay attention to the suffering of Jesus—to his emotional distress as well as his physical pain and exhaustion. Consider, then, how well he understands the suffering experienced by you and your loved ones.

DAY 39

Doing What You Love

A man must love a thing very much if he not only practices it without any hope of fame or money, but even practices it without any hope of doing it well. Such a man must love the toils of the work more than any other man can love the rewards of it.

ROBERT BROWNING

WORK AS UNTO THE LORD

> *Commit your work to the LORD,*
> *and your plans will be established.*

PROVERBS 16:3

PRAYER

Help us, Father, Son, and Holy Spirit, to do well those works you have prepared us to do. Give us courage and strength, and remind us to ask for your assistance so that we may not work in vain.

LENTEN ACTION

Can you identify one thing that you love to do but don't do particularly well? For some of us, this might be singing or dancing; for others, it might be something entirely different. Try to practice this unskilled skill of yours in a way that praises God. Sing a hymn in the shower. Dance when nobody's looking.

DAY 40

The Donkey

When fishes flew and forests walked
   And figs grew upon thorn
Some moment when the moon was blood
   Then surely I was born.

With monstrous head and sickening cry
   And ears like errant wings
The devil's walking parody
   On all four-footed things.

The tattered outlaw of the earth
   Of ancient crooked will
Starve, scourge, deride me; I am dumb
   I keep my secret still.
Fools! for I also had my hour
   One far fierce hour and sweet
There was a shout about my ears
   And palms before my feet.

COLLECTED POETRY

ENTERING THE CITY

When they had come near Jerusalem and had reached Bethphage, at the Mount of Olives, Jesus sent two disciples, saying to them, "Go into the village ahead of you, and immediately you will find a donkey tied, and a colt with her; untie them and bring them to me. If anyone says anything to you, just say this, 'The Lord needs them.' And he will send them immediately." This took place to fulfill what had been spoken through the prophet, saying,

"Tell the daughter of Zion,
Look, your king is coming to you,
humble, and mounted on a donkey,
and on a colt, the foal of a donkey."

The disciples went and did as Jesus had directed them; they brought the donkey and the colt, and put their cloaks on them, and he sat on them. A very large crowd spread their cloaks on the road, and others cut branches from the trees and spread them on the road. The crowds that went ahead of him and that followed were shouting,

"Hosanna to the Son of David!
Blessed is the one who comes in the name of the Lord!
Hosanna in the highest heaven!"

MATTHEW 21:1–9

PRAYER

Lord, how vain I am; forgive me. Help me take my eyes off myself and see more of you in the world around me. Help me accept gratefully the role you have assigned to me in this life. Give me the gift of heart and lips that praise you.

Lenten Action

As a way of meditating on your relative smallness in the grand scheme of things, study the stars on a clear night, look through a detailed timeline of human civilization, or read about the age of the earth compared with how long humans have existed on our planet. In conclusion, express in prayer that you thank and trust God for the gift of your life and vow to use your gifts more completely for God's purposes.

DAY 41

What Use Are Words?

The tale has been retold with patronizing pathos by elegant skeptics and with fluent enthusiasm by boisterous best-sellers. It will not be retold here. The grinding power of the plain words of the Gospel story is like the power of mill-stones; and those who can read them simply enough will feel as if rocks had been rolled upon them. Criticism is only words about words; and of what use are words about such words as these? What is the use of word-painting about the dark garden filled suddenly with torchlight and furious faces? "Are you come out with swords and staves as against a robber? All day I sat in your temple teaching, and you took me not." Can anything be added to the massive and gathered restraint of that irony; like a great wave lifted to the sky and refusing to fall? "Daughters of Jerusalem, weep not for me but weep for yourselves and for your children." As the High Priest asked what further need he had of witnesses, we might well ask what further need we have of words.

THE EVERLASTING MAN

HE OPENED NOT HIS MOUTH

He was oppressed, and he was afflicted,
yet he did not open his mouth;
like a lamb that is led to the slaughter,
and like a sheep that before its shearers is silent,
so he did not open his mouth.

ISAIAH 53:7

PRAYER

Lord, how often I am tempted to put others down or call attention to myself. I barely notice my underlying motives. Deliver me, God of Truth, from vain or rash words. I have often regretted words I have spoken, but seldom have I regretted my silence. Teach me to tame my tongue this week. Let the practice of silence change first my actions, then my thoughts, and finally my heart, that I might be more filled with the fruit of your Spirit.

LENTEN ACTION

There is a story from the Desert Fathers describing how a holy man kept rocks in his mouth as a way of learning the discipline of silence. Gandhi used to practice silence every Monday. Develop some way to monitor unnecessary speech this week. Perhaps you could actually count your words as a way of cutting back on chatter, or perhaps it would help to focus on listening to others instead. Read through the Passion narrative, in one sitting if possible (Mark 14–15 is the most abbreviated version). As you find yourself speaking less this week, fill your mind instead with phrases and images from the Passion story.

DAY 42

Saving the Shipwrecked

I happen to think the whole modern attitude towards beggars is entirely heathen and inhuman. I should be prepared to maintain, as a matter of general morality, that it is intrinsically indefensible to punish human beings for asking for human assistance. I should say that it is intrinsically insane to urge people to give charity and forbid people to accept charity....Everyone would expect to have to help a man to save his life in a shipwreck; why not a man who has suffered a shipwreck of his life?

Fancies Versus Fads

What I Have I Give

One day Peter and John were going up to the temple at the hour of prayer, at three o'clock in the afternoon. And a man lame from birth was being carried in. People would lay him daily at the gate of the temple called the Beautiful Gate so that he could ask for alms from those entering the temple. When he saw Peter and John about to go into the temple, he asked them for alms. Peter looked intently at him, as did John, and said, "Look at us." And he fixed his attention on them, expecting to receive something from them. But Peter said, "I have no silver or gold, but what I have I give you; in the name of Jesus Christ of Nazareth, stand up and walk." And he took him by the right hand and raised him up; and immediately his feet and ankles were made strong. Jumping up, he stood and began to walk, and he entered the temple with them, walking and leaping and praising God."

ACTS 3:1–8

PRAYER

Lord of the Lame, Healer of the Hurt, Reconciler of the Ruined, as much as we want to be loved by you, we want also to love like you. Teach us, guide us, allow us the great privilege to care for our fellow creatures, and like the lame man, we will praise you.

LENTEN ACTION

Sometimes, merely by looking for them, we see around us people who have suffered some kind of shipwreck. Be especially attentive today, and offer to one of these whatever it is you possess—your time, your talent, your money, your prayers.

DAY 43

Two Truths and a Contradiction to Boot

*M*ysticism keeps men sane. As long as you have mystery you have health; when you destroy mystery you create morbidity. The ordinary man has always been sane because the ordinary man has always been a mystic. He has permitted the twilight....He has always cared more for truth than for consistency. If he saw two truths that seemed to contradict each other, he would take the two truths and the contradiction along with them.

ORTHODOXY

A MYSTERY

Listen, I will tell you a mystery! We will not all die, but we will all be changed, in a moment, in the twinkling of an eye, at the last trumpet. For the trumpet will sound, and the dead will be raised imperishable, and we will be changed.

For this perishable body must put on imperishability, and this mortal body must put on immortality.

1 CORINTHIANS 15:51–53

PRAYER

Gladly we live in this mystery, O Heavenly Father, and we thank you for the promise of immortality. When it suits you, change us; contradict our flesh with a heavenly body, for we hope only in what we know through the resurrection of Christ—that eternal life with you awaits us.

LENTEN ACTION

One of the most uplifting works of art is Handel's *The Messiah*. Set aside some time this week to listen to it.

DAY 44

The God Who Forsakes Himself

I approach a matter more dark and awful than it is easy to discuss; and I apologize in advance if any of my phrases fall wrong or seem irreverent touching a matter which the greatest saints and thinkers have justly feared to approach. But in that terrific tale of the Passion there is a distinct emotional suggestion that the author of all things (in some unthinkable way) went not only through agony, but through doubt. It is written, "Thou shalt not tempt the Lord thy God." No; but the Lord thy God may tempt Himself; and it seems as if this was what happened in Gethsemane. In a garden Satan tempted man: and in a garden God tempted God. He passed in some superhuman manner through our human horror of pessimism. When the world shook and the sun was wiped out of heaven, it was not at the crucifixion, but at the cry from the cross; the cry which confessed that God was forsaken of God. And now let the revolutionists choose a creed from all the creeds and a god from all the gods of the world, carefully weighing all the gods of inevitable recurrence and unalterable power. They will not find another god who has himself been in revolt. Nay (the matter grows too difficult for human speech), but let the atheists themselves choose a god. They will find only one divinity who ever uttered their isolation; only one religion in which God seemed for an instant to be an atheist.

ORTHODOXY

DARKNESS OVER ALL THE LAND

From noon on, darkness came over the whole land until three in the afternoon. And about three o'clock Jesus cried with a loud voice, "Eli, Eli, lema sabachthani?" that is, "My God, my God, why have you forsaken me?"

MATTHEW 27:45–46

PRAYER

Even doubt, even abandonment, you suffered, Lord Jesus Christ. To be fully human, you took these and added them to your physical torture. You went beyond what any human would ask of God; being God and human, you were more, and suffered more, and gave more—and all for our sake.

HOLY THURSDAY ACTION

Make plans now to say a special prayer tomorrow (Good Friday) at 3:00 PM. Choose a place where you can go alone or with a group to say a prayer thanking Christ for his sacrifice and suffering.

DAY 45

Soul and Body

The greatest act of faith that a man can perform is the act we perform every night. We abandon our identity, we turn our soul and body into chaos and old night. We uncreate ourselves as if at the end of the world: for all practical purposes we become dead men, in the sure and certain hope of a glorious resurrection.

LUNACY AND LETTERS

INTO YOUR HANDS

It was now about noon, and darkness came over the whole land until three in the afternoon, while the sun's light failed; and the curtain of the temple was torn in two. Then Jesus, crying with a loud voice, said, "Father, into your hands I commend my spirit."

LUKE 23:44–46

PRAYER

Heavenly Father, teach us to see in the dark, as your Son did during his darkest moment on earth. Give us spiritual eyes, that we might see you and commend our spirits to you. Let us not forget the promise of resurrection.

GOOD FRIDAY ACTION

Many churches have Good Friday vigils during which members volunteer to stay up throughout the night, taking turns keeping watch. If your church has such a program, consider signing up. If not, try saying your evening prayers in the dark tonight, perhaps outside. Hold the hope that is within you against the darkness that is before you. Recall Chesterton's words that we have a "sure and certain hope of a glorious resurrection." Recall these words once more in the morning when you see the first sign of light.

DAY 46

Miracles

The most incredible thing about miracles is that they happen.

THE FATHER BROWN OMNIBUS

THEY REMEMBERED

But on the first day of the week, at early dawn, they came to the tomb, taking the spices that they had prepared. They found the stone rolled away from the tomb, but when they went in, they did not find the body. While they were perplexed about this, suddenly two men in dazzling clothes stood beside them. The women were terrified and bowed their faces to the ground, but the men said to them, "Why do you look for the living among the dead? He is not here, but has risen. Remember how he told you, while he was still in Galilee, that the Son of Man must be handed over to sinners, and be crucified, and on the third day rise again."

Then they remembered his words, and returning from the tomb, they told all this to the eleven and to all the rest.

LUKE 24:1–9

PRAYER

God of Miracles, open our eyes to the resurrection of your Son. Though thousands of years separate us from this event, may it be to us as if it happened today, and as if we ourselves are there.

HOLY SATURDAY ACTION

When you answer the phone tomorrow, say "Happy Easter" or "The Lord is risen!"

PART II

~~~~~~

READINGS *for* EASTER

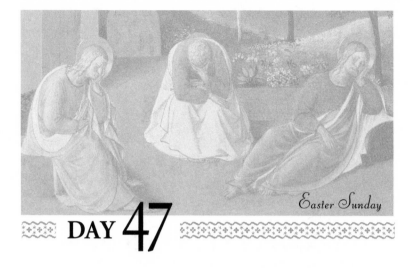

DAY 47

The Promise of Resurrection

*C*hrist is the Sun of Easter" does not mean that the worshipper is praising the sun under the emblem of Christ. Goddess or god can clothe themselves with the spring or summer; but the body is more than raiment. Religion takes almost disdainfully the dress of Nature; and indeed Christianity has done as well with the snows of Christmas as with the snow-drops of spring. And when I look across the sun-struck fields, I know in my inmost bones that my joy is not solely in the spring, for spring alone, being always returning, would be always sad. There is somebody or something walking there, to be crowned with flowers: and my pleasure is in some promise yet possible and in the resurrection of the dead.

A MISCELLANY OF MEN

THE GARDENER

But Mary stood weeping outside the tomb. As she wept, she bent over to look into the tomb; and she saw two angels in white, sitting where the body of Jesus had been lying, one at the head and the other at the feet. They said to her, "Woman, why are you weeping?" She said to them, "They have taken away my Lord, and I do not know where they have laid him." When she had said this, she turned around and saw Jesus standing there, but she did not know that it was Jesus. Jesus said to her, "Woman, why are you weeping? Whom are you looking for?" Supposing him to be the gardener, she said to him, "Sir, if you have carried him away, tell me where you have laid him, and I will take him away." Jesus said to her, "Mary!" She turned and said to him in Hebrew, "Rabbouni!" (which means Teacher). Jesus said to her, "Do not hold on to me, because I have not yet ascended to the Father. But go to my brothers and say to them, 'I am ascending to my Father and your Father, to my God and your God.'" Mary Magdalene went and announced to the disciples, "I have seen the Lord"; and she told them that he had said these things to her.

JOHN 20:11–18

PRAYER

Lord, may the hope of resurrection never dull my duty to act as a good steward of the gifts you have entrusted to me. Deliver me from apathetically waiting for you to accomplish outside of history restoration that you would have me accomplish within my life. May your resurrection power—to redeem and restore a broken creation—be unleashed in and through me. Your kingdom come, your will be done.

EASTER ACTION

Sketch an abstract picture using only three circles or curves, seven lines, four rectangles, and one triangle. Use only pencil or charcoal if possible. Do not spend much more than a few minutes on your drawing. Having finished it, imagine now that this set of geometric shapes is a message of God's promise to you of hope, and spend some time interpreting it. What communication of encouragement can you read in these lines?

DAY 48

The Softness of Mud

The real distinction between the ethics of high art and the ethics of manufactured and didactic art lies in the simple fact that the bad fable has a moral, while the good fable is a moral. And the real moral of Tolstoy comes out constantly in these stories, the great moral which lies at the heart of all his work, of which he is probably unconscious, and of which it is quite likely that he would vehemently disapprove. The curious cold white light of morning that shines over all the tales, the folklore simplicity with which "a man or a woman" are spoken of without further identification, the love—one might almost say the lust—for the qualities of brute materials, the hardness of wood, and the softness of mud, the ingrained belief in a certain ancient kindliness sitting beside the very cradle of the race of man—these influences are truly moral.

TWELVE TYPES

The Word Became Flesh

And the Word became flesh and lived among us, and we have seen his glory, the glory as of a father's only son, full of grace and truth.

JOHN 1:14

We declare to you what was from the beginning, what we have heard, what we have seen with our eyes, what we have looked at and touched with our hands, concerning the word of life—this life was revealed, and we have seen it and testify to it, and declare to you the eternal life that was with the Father and was revealed to us—we declare to you what we have seen and heard so that you also may have fellowship with us; and truly our fellowship is with the Father and with his Son Jesus Christ. We are writing these things so that our joy may be complete.

1 JOHN 1:1–4

Prayer

Thank you, Lord, for the beauty and wonder of your world—for the hardness of wood and the softness of mud, for the briskness of cold and the wetness of water. Thank you for the life you've granted us—for the satisfaction of good work done and for the softness of sheets at the end of the day. Let me see you in all things and love you above all things.

EASTER ACTION

Go for a short rambling walk outside today. Ask God to
speak through your senses. Be alive to sounds and smells.
Do something outside—feel rain on your face, wind in
your hair, mud on your fingers; smell the spring earth, the
flowers, the grass; listen to the sounds of water, of birds.
Imagine these sensory experiences as God's direct signs
of love to you—his tender touch, his gentle caress.

DAY 49

A New Day Dawns

On the third day the friends of Christ coming at daybreak to the place found the grave empty and the stone rolled away. In varying ways they realized the new wonder; but even they hardly realized that the world had died in the night. What they were looking at was the first day of a new creation, with a new heaven and a new earth; and in a semblance of the gardener God walked again in the garden, in the cool not of the evening but the dawn.

THE EVERLASTING MAN

THE FIRST DAY DAWNING

After the sabbath, as the first day of the week was dawning, Mary Magdalene and the other Mary went to see the tomb. And suddenly there was a great earthquake; for an angel of the Lord, descending from heaven, came and rolled back the stone and sat on it. His appearance was like lightning, and his clothing white as snow. For fear of him the guards shook and became like dead men. But the angel said to the women, "Do not be afraid; I know that you are looking for Jesus who was crucified. He is not here; for he has been raised, as he said. Come, see the place where he lay. Then go quickly and tell his disciples, 'He has been raised from the dead, and indeed he is going ahead of you to Galilee; there you will see him.' This is my message for you." So they left the tomb quickly with fear and great joy, and ran to tell his disciples. Suddenly Jesus met them and said, "Greetings!" And they came to him, took hold of his feet, and worshiped him. Then Jesus said to them, "Do not be afraid; go and tell my brothers to go to Galilee; there they will see me."

MATTHEW 28:1–10

PRAYER

God, renew my sense of your presence—like a new friend whom I am excited to meet again, converse with, and just sit beside. Make my soul thirsty for you, thirstier than for those things that promise to make me happy but leave me only more parched in the end. Lord, do something new in me.

EASTER ACTION

Do something in your garden (or in a friend's garden): rake, till, trim, or plant bulbs or annuals. Touch and smell the earth, the grass and greenery, and appreciate their earthiness, their greenness. As you do, imaginatively contemplate God in Christ—the Creator of All—freshly risen from the grave and walking in your garden.

Wednesday of Easter Week

DAY 50

The Humility to Imagine

*I*t is not bigotry to be certain we are right; but it is bigotry to be unable to imagine how we might possibly have gone wrong.

THE CATHOLIC CHURCH AND CONVERSION

A WEEK LATER

But Thomas (who was called the Twin), one of the twelve, was not with them when Jesus came. So the other disciples told him, "We have seen the Lord." But he said to them, "Unless I see the mark of the nails in his hands, and put my finger in the mark of the nails and my hand in his side, I will not believe." A week later his disciples were again in the house, and Thomas was with them. Although the doors were shut, Jesus came and stood among them and said, "Peace be with you." Then he said to Thomas, "Put your finger here and see my hands. Reach out your hand and put it in my side. Do not doubt but believe." Thomas answered him, "My Lord and my God!"

JOHN 20:24–28

PRAYER

Lord Jesus, help us in our unbelief. Like Thomas, we sometimes cannot fathom your miracles until you stand miraculously before us. Have mercy on us. Speak to us in your gentle voice. Forgive our probing fingers.

EASTER ACTION

Read the first twenty-three verses of John 20, and try to imagine how you would have responded if you were Thomas and heard the astonishing news that the other disciples brought. Through the power of the imagination, try to put yourself in his place. How would you have responded to Christ's invitation to touch his wounds?

DAY 51

A Love of Special Places

$\mathcal{I}$ think God has given us the love of special places, of a hearth and of a native land, for a good reason....I mean...that if there be a house for me in heaven it will either have a green lamp-post and a hedge, or something quite as positive and personal as a green lamp-post and a hedge. I mean that God bade me love one spot and serve it, and do all things however wild in praise of it, so that this one spot might be a witness against all the infinities and the sophistries, that Paradise is somewhere and not anywhere, is something and not anything."

SMITH, QUOTED IN *MANALIVE*

GOD'S HOME AMONG MORTALS

Then I saw a new heaven and a new earth; for the first heaven and the first earth had passed away, and the sea was no more. And I saw the holy city, the new Jerusalem, coming down out of heaven from God, prepared as a bride adorned for her husband. And I heard a loud voice from the throne saying,

> *"See, the home of God is among mortals.*
> *He will dwell with them as their God;*
> *they will be his peoples,*
> *and God himself will be with them."*

REVELATION 21:1–3

PRAYER

Lord of Earth and of Heaven, thank you for the goodness of creation. Everything that you made is good. Remind us today as we encounter the particular geographical place in which we find ourselves that you made all things, that you sustain all things, and that you love all things. Let us share your love for this earth, for this place, for our home and our hearth.

EASTER ACTION

Practice spiritual reading *(lectio divina)* of nature today. Take an outdoor walk with your senses alert and activated. Follow these four steps: read, reflect, respond, and rest. First, select some particular object near where you live and "read" it, study it, drink it in. If the weather is inclement, find something portable to bring inside—a flower, leaf, stone, or twig. After careful observation, "reflect" spiritually—meditate on nature's intricacy and design, on its shape and beauty, on its spiritually symbolic significance for your life right now. What is God saying to you through what you have surveyed? Consider any Scripture that comes to mind or any spiritual lessons. After spending some time in reflective meditation, begin to "respond" by using your reflection as a springboard for prayer, praising and thanking God and offering God your most intimate thoughts and concerns. Finally, "rest." At this point, you do not need more information. Simply sit silently in God's presence for several minutes. End by slowly praying aloud the Lord's Prayer.

DAY 52

Dancing Legs

*I*t is often said by the critics of Christian origins that certain ritual feasts, processions or dances are really of pagan origin. They might as well say that our legs are of pagan origin....One of the chief claims of Christian civilization is to have preserved things of pagan origin. In short, in the old religious countries men *continue* to dance; while in the new scientific cities they are often content to drudge.

THE SUPERSTITION OF DIVORCE

A DANCE BEFORE THE LORD

David danced before the LORD with all his might....David and all the house of Israel brought up the ark of the LORD with shouting, and with the sound of the trumpet.

2 SAMUEL 6:14–15

PRAYER

Lord of the Dance and of all holy celebration, thank you for the joy we feel in our bodies. We are grateful that we can express this joy to you in a dance or a song or a simple smile.

EASTER ACTION

Choose a favorite hymn and sing it alone or with a group.

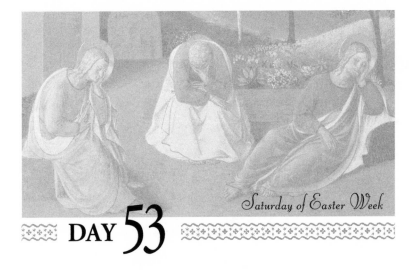

DAY 53

The Realism of Love

assion makes every detail important; there is no realism like the insatiable realism of love.

"BROWNING AND HIS IDEAL," *A HANDFUL OF AUTHORS: ESSAYS ON BOOKS AND WRITERS*

ATTENTION TO DETAIL

Meanwhile, standing near the cross of Jesus were his mother, and his mother's sister, Mary the wife of Clopas, and Mary Magdalene. When Jesus saw his mother and the disciple whom he loved standing beside her, he said to his mother, "Woman, here is your son." Then he said to the disciple, "Here is your mother." And from that hour the disciple took her into his own home.

JOHN 19:25–27

PRAYER

Dear Jesus, we are moved by this story. Even while suffering, you remembered your mother and made arrangements for her. Teach us to pay such close attention to others, even when our own pain might easily distract us.

EASTER ACTION

Choose a family member and do a kind thing for that person.

DAY 54

The Mystery

If sunset clouds could grow on trees
   It would but match the may in flower;
And skies be underneath the seas
No topsyturvier than a shower.

If mountains rose on wings to wander
They were no wilder than a cloud;
Yet all my praise is mean as slander,
Mean as these mean words spoken aloud.

And never more than now I know
That man's first heaven is far behind;
Unless the blazing seraph's blow
Has left him in the garden blind.

Witness, O Sun that blinds our eyes,
Unthinkable and unthankable King,
That though all other wonder dies
I wonder at not wondering.

COLLECTED POETRY

THINGS TOO WONDERFUL

Then Job answered the LORD:
 "I know that you can do all things,
 and that no purpose of yours can be thwarted.
 'Who is this that hides counsel without knowledge?'
 Therefore I have uttered what I did not understand,
 things too wonderful for me, which I did not know."

JOB 42:1–3

PRAYER

Lord, how easily I forget. Help me remember what you have done for me in Christ. Help me remember the means of grace you offer me through your Church. Lord, how quickly I grow bored. Wake me to the wonder of your well-fashioned world. Lord, how often I plod along with the eyes of my soul either shut or downcast, indifferent to the needs of those around me. Give me eyes of compassion to see others as you would.

EASTER ACTION

Take a rambling, "wondering" walk today, noticing things you often take for granted and marveling at what seems to startle or amaze, and thank God for creating and sustaining all things in the universe with such love.

*S*ources and *A*cknowledgments

The Collected Works of G. K. Chesterton, an ongoing project published by Ignatius Press, attempts to make available in one
source all of Chesterton's published writings. At present, the
series includes thirty-five volumes and foresees an additional
ten. Material excerpted for this book can be found in that ex-
cellent series, with the exception of the following:

Chesterton, G. K. *All Is Grist.* North Stratford, NH: Ayer Com-
pany Publishers, 2000. Used with permission of A P Watt Ltd.
on behalf of The Royal Literary Fund.

————. *The Autobiography of G. K. Chesterton.* New York: Sheed
and Ward, 1936. Used with permission of A P Watt Ltd. on
behalf of The Royal Literary Fund.

————. *Avowals and Denials.* New York: Dodd, Mead and Co.,
1935. Used with permission of A P Watt Ltd. on behalf of The
Royal Literary Fund.

————. *The Catholic Church and Conversion.* New York: Mac-
millan Co., 1951. Used with permission of A P Watt Ltd. on
behalf of The Royal Literary Fund.

————. *The Everlasting Man.* New York: Dodd, Mead and Co.,
1925. Used with permission of A P Watt Ltd. on behalf of The
Royal Literary Fund.

————. *Fancies Versus Fads.* New York: Dodd, Mead and Co.,
1923. Used with permission of A P Watt Ltd. on behalf of The
Royal Literary Fund.

————. *The Father Brown Omnibus.* New York: Dodd, Mead and
Co., 1951. Used with permission of A P Watt Ltd. on behalf of
The Royal Literary Fund.

————. *Generally Speaking.* New York: Dodd, Mead and Co., 1929. Used with permission of A P Watt Ltd. on behalf of The Royal Literary Fund.

————. *G. F. Watts.* London: Duckworth, 1975.

————. *G. K. C. as M. C.* Ed. J. P. de Fonseka. London: Methuen, 1929. Used with permission of A P Watt Ltd. on behalf of The Royal Literary Fund.

————. *A Handful of Authors: Essays on Books and Writers.* New York: Sheed and Ward, 1953.

————. "Introduction to the Book of Job." In *G. K. C. as M. C.,* edited by J. P. de Fonseka. London: Methuen, 1929, 34–52. Used with permission of A P Watt Ltd. on behalf of The Royal Literary Fund.

————. *Lunacy and Letters.* New York: Sheed and Ward, 1958.

————. *A Miscellany of Men.* Norfolk, VA: IHS Press, 2004.

————. *Twelve Types.* Norfolk, VA: IHS Press, 2003.

————. *The Way of the Cross,* in *Collected Works,* Vol. III. San Francisco: Ignatius, 1990, 535–549. Used with permission of A P Watt Ltd. on behalf of The Royal Literary Fund.